Whispering Soul

Love Quotes

SOPHIE A. LILLE

Whispering Soul
Copyright © 2022 by Sophie A. Lille

All rights reserved. No part of this publication may be reproduced, distributed, or transmitted in any form or by any means, including photocopying, recording, or other electronic or mechanical methods, without the prior written permission of the author, except in the case of brief quotations embodied in critical reviews and certain other non-commercial uses permitted by copyright law.

Tellwell Talent
www.tellwell.ca

ISBN
978-0-2288-7344-0 (Hardcover)
978-0-2288-7343-3 (Paperback)

ACKNOWLEDGEMENT

I would like to express my gratitude towards all my family, friends and my life journey that has taken me to this point in my existence with much guidance, knowledge and support, that has given me the courage and confidence in creating my "Soul Purpose" in sharing with you all.

My special thanks and appreciation to all my colleagues in helping me with my computer skills making my book possible.

I would also like to give special thanks to Scott Lunn and Sem Delima at "Tell Well Publications" with their expertise making this all possible for me, it has truly been an amazing journey

DEDICATION

My dedication going to the love of my life, my best friend, who keeps me focused, supports and believes in me, allowing me to follow and pursue my hopes and dreams

TABLE OF CONTENTS

Taking Control Of Your Life	1
Forgiveness	2
Giving Up	3
Dreams	4
Desire	6
Fear	7
Fate Was Chosen	8
My Forever Love	9
Secret To Life	11
Broken Children	12
Setting Them Up For Failure	13
Needing A Friend	14
Kindness	15
Promise	16
Hidden	17
New Day	18
Truth Wins	19
Brave	21
Energy	22
Life	23
Balance	24
One Of A Kind	25
Grati Tude	26
Energy Is Everything	29
You're Not Alone	30
Putting Karma To Rest	31
Forgiveness To Oneself	32
My Journey	33

Waiting	34
My Unknown Heart	35
Never Stop Doing The Little Things	37
You're Not Alone	39
Under The Sun	40
The Real Thing	42
Land Of Indecission	44
Be The Change	45
Lifes Great Risks	46
Purpose	47
Black Tunnel	48
Tear Drops	49
Lea P Of Faith	50
The Love I Have	51
Your Lingering Touch	52
Butterfly Love	55
If I Were Ever To Lose Your Love	56
Faint Silence	58
Casting The Line	59
Two Minds Alike	61
Cycles In Life	62
A Bridge	63
Fathers Wisdom	64
Whispering Soul	65
Keepsake	66

TAKING CONTROL OF YOUR LIFE

We all go through periods in our daily lives

Where things get chaotic and we feel overwhelmed or like we are falling behind.

It soon falls into place

Getting back on track and regaining a sense of direction that we all go through in our daily lives.

Know that this will pass and you will then gain the control that is needed

Moving forward, and taking the actions that are necessary

FORGIVENESS

How much space does the word "forgiveness" take up in your life?

Have you ever found it difficult to forgive someone?

Are there things or people you feel like you will never forgive?

I found that journal writing became an excellent way to get perspective, practicing love and forgiveness

Transcending all suffering and move into a space of profound joy, peace, and harmony in every moment

GIVING UP

A time wanting to give up

A feeling you cannot

A path you feel and must pursue

Always in your head

Looking for answers before you

Looking for hope

Then something comes around

When you least expect

Realizing you're on the right path.

DREAMS

Dreams may come and go

Remember you can make anything happen

You set your mind too

Hard work is needed along with much patience.

Our dreams may sometimes

Be not as realistic as we think or as our friends feel it should be

Have no fear

Believe in the impossible

It shall be yours

Setting a strong plan and goal

Not letting time be a factor

Time and place will come

What is meant for you

Never let anyone tell you differently

There will always be haters

There will be people who will bring you to your knees

Always remember your dreams

Your journey and yours only

If you're granted a partner or friend to fill that dream together

It will be worth that much more

Connected with one another throwing ideas back and forth

Making the dream or dreams come into fruition

We as humans have the capability to pursue our hopes and dreams whatever that may be

After all we would not be our true authentic selves or living our full lives without our dreams.....

Share with others

Giving them the courage

That they too can make their dreams come true.....

DESIRE

Ask one selves

What is it that I truly desire?

You have the power to have anything you want

By being your true authentic self

Not allowing to be influenced by others

Be free

Not the one being held in a cage

Dreamland desires will be yours

Time to step in your power and make them possible

FEAR

Some people are so invested in fear

Peace becomes a threatening issue more than you can imagine

FATE WAS CHOSEN

From the moment I first saw you

All my darkness turned to light

A rare and priceless work of art

I'm here by your side

Standing in front of a masterpiece

The pain I endure to be so in love with you

To be the chosen one

With all the ups and downs

Fate was chosen

Our love being indestructible

MY FOREVER LOVE

Know my love was pure

Everything was meant to be

We were blessed

Finding one another

A true love

A best friend

Although you may not see me

Know I'm watching over you

Along with our wonderful boys too

My body may not be next to you

My very soul surrounds you day and night

I'm safe up above

I'm the sun in the horizon

As in the clouds a silver lining

Do not weep my precious love

You need to be strong in continuing what we started together

That I cannot

When you need my help

Call my name and I shall be there

Through the faint whisper I call to you

I'm never far away

For I'm always by your side

One day you will see the light through the tunnel as I did

I will be on the other side waiting for you

Joining me re-connecting once again as we were once before

Yours Truly

My Forever Love

SECRET TO LIFE

Life is a series of many tiny miracles

Before you

Create the life you want within

Follow it........

BROKEN CHILDREN

Living, mimicking adult lives

Giving to the future generation before us

Giving strength, direction and love that's needed

Not molding our insecurities onto these little innocent angels

SETTING THEM UP FOR FAILURE

Need to prepare them to what the future lies ahead

Life may not always be perfect

It's you that that will make life what you want it to be

NEEDING A FRIEND

I can't promise to solve your problems

What I can promise
Is that you won't ever have to face alone

I promise I will always be here for you
This being my promise to you

KINDNESS

Everyone you meet

Is battling some kind of problem

You may not know of

Don't make judgement

Be kind

PROMISE

I promise I will share all of my feelings with you. [Even if it's hard to do]

I promise I will always be considerate of your feelings [even if you're wrong]

I promise I will always be honest with you [even if I have to pay for the consequences for my actions]

I promise I will always laugh [even if I'm sad]

I promise to shed my tears [even if my makeup runs]

I promise to share everything with you [even my deepest fears]

Most of all

I promise I will never stop loving you. Forever and ever......

My promise to you

HIDDEN

Inside every person you know

There is someone you don't

As humans we have fear of showing our true selves

Fear of judgement that will be made

Get past what others may think as this will stagnate you

From the doors opening before you

Bringing endless opportunities and happiness you truly deserve

NEW DAY

Everyday holds a new magic

Embrace and be grateful of all that surrounds you

Here today, tomorrow and years to come

TRUTH WINS

A very long painful path must go

Standing tall

Standing strong

Feeling very much alone

With her faith, her beliefs and dignity

She just has a knowing, in her heart

Truth will be hers Truth always win

As she continues on her path

With much strength

Being judged by many

Coworkers, friends and yes even family members

Standing in her power takes no notice.

Because......

Truth is love

Love is unconditional

Truth always wins

BRAVE

Sometimes the bravest thing we can do

Is never look back?

Did it

Done it

Lived it

And loved it

ENERGY

Be the energy you want to feel

LIFE

Life is the art of holding on

And sometimes letting go

Both being sometimes extremely difficult but necessary for one's growth

BALANCE

Sometimes it's ok to lose the balance when its one who we love

The tricky part is staying true to one's self

This then helps you to balance

Keep your mind in silence

Your heart opened

It will guide you where you to be

ONE OF A KIND

Be yourself

Your own unique self

Your own path

Will never be anyone else's

Uniqueness your blueprint

Yours only

It will never be taken from you....

Share it willingly and lovingly to all that surrounds you

GRATITUDE

I say here today and every day of my waking life

Much gratitude I have
Through much pain I've endured with ignorance

I've also gained laughter and wisdom

With my heart I've gained love and compassion

My journey in this life time
I have struggled fiercely

Finding the right path
With many forks to choose from
Finding one today that may change tomorrow

I love intensely
I know it was destined for me

A wakeup call from the higher power

Giving me the strength for what comes before me

Without these lessons I have been taught

My path would have been full of darkness, regret and despair

I have a purpose

I must be open

To the endless possibilities that the higher power has for me

Open in my heart space

Using my third eye wisely

Staying focused

Gaining the knowledge of downloads before me

Helping and teaching
Giving to others who cross my path

Having much gratitude

Loving who I have become
Loving what I can bring and share

ENERGY IS EVERYTHING

Energy you bring forth

Is being responsible you bring into a room

No time for peoples BS

Only having space for clear, positivizes around me at all times

My time is limited here

I choose to make it wisely

YOU'RE NOT ALONE

To every moment you lose hope

Your loved one is gently whispering.....

I Love You

PUTTING KARMA TO REST

Karma I brought into this life

From previous ones

Being two sides to everything in the universe

Is my karma

I am building with my words and deeds in this lifetime

This can be changed by the lessons I am supposed to be taught by each event that enters my life

The instant karma in this life time is for me to learn from the mistakes of others

This helping to guide my path through my life today

FORGIVENESS TO ONESELF

I forgive others

Does not mean I totally trust them

I forgive

As it's the right way to be

Forgiveness allows me to let go

Moving forward in continuing my journey

A path that was put before me

MY JOURNEY

Has brought me far as I continue in trusting the path I'm on

I must not take the wrong fork in the road

I've come this far

With pain, tears and tribulations

Soon before me

Laughter came too

Bringing me to a peaceful place within

This journey has truly brought the light clear before me than I could have ever imagined

I say to you

Believe …..

It too will come clear for you ….

WAITING

Is a true sign of "True Love?"

And patience

You can say "I Love You"

But not everyone is able to

Wait and prove it

MY UNKNOWN HEART

Do I open my door to let you in?

Do I tell you about all my pain and fears?

Would you not judge me if you know

What lies within my very soul?

Do I tell all the things I've

Never told anyone?

Would you think less of me?

Would you be any different than those that have come before?

The unknown can't show us how

As we search with our hearts

The unknown can't give us the answers we seek

The unknown mysteries of life show us where to start

Do I trust you enough to let you sleep next to me?

Would you hold me in your arms and keep me safe every night?

Do I give my body and soul to you?

When I awake would you still be here tomorrow?

Do I? And if I? Would you?

I will allow fate too decide...

NEVER STOP DOING THE LITTLE THINGS

Busy in our daily lives

Surrounding us with getting

Things done that need our attention

Whether its meeting deadlines at work, keeping up with paying our daily bills or attending to family obligations

The importance also is our loved ones

That we care for

Are sometimes taken for granted

We don't do this intentionally

Getting distracted from our daily lives is all

Needing to find the balance can be difficult

Remembering at the end of the day our loved ones are by your side

We need to never stop doing the little things

Whatever that is to you

Big or small

Your loved ones will always keep that close to their hearts

YOU'RE NOT ALONE

To every moment

You lose hope

Your loved one is gently

Whispering .....

UNDER THE SUN

I know what it is like behind those eyes

A pile of broken pieces that fell from your heart

There's never no escaping

Everything can change day to day

Under the sun

Remember what's done is done

Never giving up

No matter hard it seems

Hold onto your dreams as I have

There's so much love that surrounds you, still and

So much has yet to come

I know how you must feel

To those where you stand today

Feeling time passing us by

That is wasted and

Just maybe things will turn

Hoping of not getting burned once again

I say to you

Hold strong

Look around

You're not the only one

You are a light under the sun

Tomorrow is a new day

Lessons thrown on you

Stay strong

Open your heart

Tables soon will turn

Love will be yours once again

THE REAL THING

Do anything

Your wish is my command

You take my heart

You take my soul

You hold the key that bonds

These two very souls

Words don't express how you make me feel

I've sacrificed for this love

You are the sweetest song

I sing each day

The cloud I am when you are down

You, my special love

The love you give me

I build on hope

You having the power that keeps me hanging on

You have the best version of me
Then you ever had before

You, always close to my heart
At times of being so far apart
Giving you the time that's needed
Seems to have taken forever
Never will it be too late
This I feel is our fate

You are everything to me
Giving me a taste of love
You're the only one who had
The power to keep me holding on

LAND OF INDECISSION

Sitting alone in isolation

Looking into the past

Disconnected, detached emotionally and cold

Asking oneself ....

I'm needing guidance now before me

In Nomads Land being confused

Strategizing my next move

Or will I be too late?

BE THE CHANGE

This is probably the hardest thing for us to accept

Is that life owes us nothing

Not wealth

Not the perfect love

Not comfort at any time

What it provides us is raw materials

That being

For anything we wish to create

A gift of change

You and only you can create

LIFES GREAT RISKS

Remember with great love and achievements

It involves taking a great risk ....

Throughout your daily life

Be sure to be kind, smile a mostly give gratitude

Be the one who makes that someone's special day

PURPOSE

My greatest attribute

Is making those around me happy daily

Making a difference

Is what I love and feel I must do

BLACK TUNNEL

Darkness going through it

Coming out on the other side will be bright

We all have to make changes at some point in our lives

Some being easier than others

You will get past it

Work in progress

Rewards you will be granted being all worth it in the end

See you on the other side

TEAR DROPS

To those who have many teardrops

And to those who don't

LEAP OF FAITH

Take that leap with me

Going after our dreams as one

Let's make it happen

Living with no regrets my love

Believing we can and we will

THE LOVE I HAVE

My attitude in check

Forgiveness is a must

Be above

The ones who have hurt you

They may be too weak to apologize for what they have done

All we can hope for

Is those who have done you wrong

They find the strength in doing the right thing and finding peace within

YOUR LINGERING TOUCH

Overcoming obstacles

That prevent us from moving forward

Going through a turbulent funk

Karma before me

I'm the eye in the middle of a storm

I must resolve turbulent issues before me

Being a people pleaser

Keeping me stuck

Judgement is mine

Lessons I now must face

A lot of feelings and emotions I have towards you

My mask on

I keep hidden from the surface

Hidden in Truth

Suffering inside

My heart and soul is going through major life changes

A knowing I can't explain

A yearning and longing for you

This connection we have has not been an easy nor was it meant to be

Lessons thrown my way

Lessons I must face

A test of fate I feel

Challenges I must face and be washed away

My respect and love I have for you

I put you on a pedestal

I lay it on the line one day

Wanting you to see clearly

What it was I was going through

Love you so much

I loved to not burden on you

Saving and protecting I could not allow you to go through the darkness I have endured

I ask of you to please forgive me

Keeping it a secret

Doing what I felt was best

Feeling your lingering touch

Know I'm coming home to you

When the time is right

When the time be ours

BUTTERFLY LOVE

My love is pure

My love is kind

My love is not always patient

My stomach

Begins to flutter ......

Like a butterfly it comes and goes as it pleases

With love it brings

I reach over to you

Looking into your eyes

My lashes

Begin to flutter with butterfly kisses I must not pass you by

IF I WERE EVER TO LOSE YOUR LOVE

Waiting all my love life playing my cards right

Should I lose this love

Or if you turned away

Saying goodbye

How do

I go on?

The pain so great

Of holding on too tight

Not being good at this

My heart so fragile

Staggering on the edge

No wishing well will suffice

Finding better things in life

Still getting by

The pain I would face

Would tear me apart if I were to ever lose your love

FAINT SILENCE

My whispering soul in the faint distance

I call to you

Being silenced for many years

Feeling at times

My existence

Not being heard

CASTING THE LINE

The waters are rough

Treading steadily beneath the ocean floor

Waters are calm now

Time has come

He sets out to sail with all good intentions

A safe place he feels

Alone

A place he can go within

On clear smooth waters

He casts his line

Seeing a reflection, a silhouette of his and mine

Beneath him

Lies fears of the unknown

He wheels his catch in
Much pride he displays

Throwing back to dark waters before him
Setting if free....
Casting the line that cannot ever break

Soon another time will be his
Once smooth waters arise
Will be his to take

TWO MINDS ALIKE

A different kind of intimacy

You understanding my mind

Keeping soothing my soul

Is all you must do and you will have all of me forever more

CYCLES IN LIFE

In life we go through many cycles

Much like the four seasons

Some seasons better than others

Depending on what transitions we may be going through in that particular space and time

Though challenging times ....

Know it's a cycle and soon it will pass

Acceptance is needed

A BRIDGE

In quiet solitude I claim

Checking in on my gifts

Respecting my intuition

Being important for me in practicing random acts of kindness

Holding space for them in offering hope

In any other way I can assist

Help and heal the world in need

FATHERS WISDOM

My father always said

Question where your loyalties lie

The people you trust will expect it

Your greatest enemies will desire it

Those you treasure the most

Will without fail

Will abuse it

WHISPERING SOUL

Your soul will always whisper your truth
Wanting the very best for you

Never silent the whisper it shares

Long periods of time
Will sure to build up
Making it difficult to say your truth

Those around you trying to understand
Eventually will roar back at you

KEEPSAKE

- ∞ Life is the art of holding on and sometimes of letting go
- ∞ What is meant to be, will always find its way
- ∞ Negative events are sticky, they leave me feeling drained
- ∞ Why not focus on positivity
- ∞ Surrendering, doing the work and accepting
- ∞ Knowing your purpose, standing strong in it and you will be protected
- ∞ Silence is needed to go within
- ∞ Free will, to be chosen to teach truth
- ∞ Generous, people have more to give
- ∞ Freedom always follows
- ∞ Truth will set you free
- ∞ Fight for your dreams and your dreams become your reality

- ∞ Obstacles don't block your path, they are the path
- ∞ Fear destroys, lose the fear and you will become whatever you want to be
- ∞ Powerful mind is everything, remember, what you think you become
- ∞ My faint whisper is always present, you just have to listen

Even if at a distance

www.ingramcontent.com/pod-product-compliance
Lightning Source LLC
LaVergne TN
LVHW011739060526
838200LV00051B/3250